MY PET
SNAKE

MATT REHER
& LIAM HANSEN–THIIM

I live here.

This is my snake.

3

I live here with my snake.

My snake is my pet!

This is the sun.

All snakes have to have sun.

Lots of snakes get sun like this.

HEAT LAMP

My snake can't do that.
He gets sun like this.

9

All snakes have to eat.

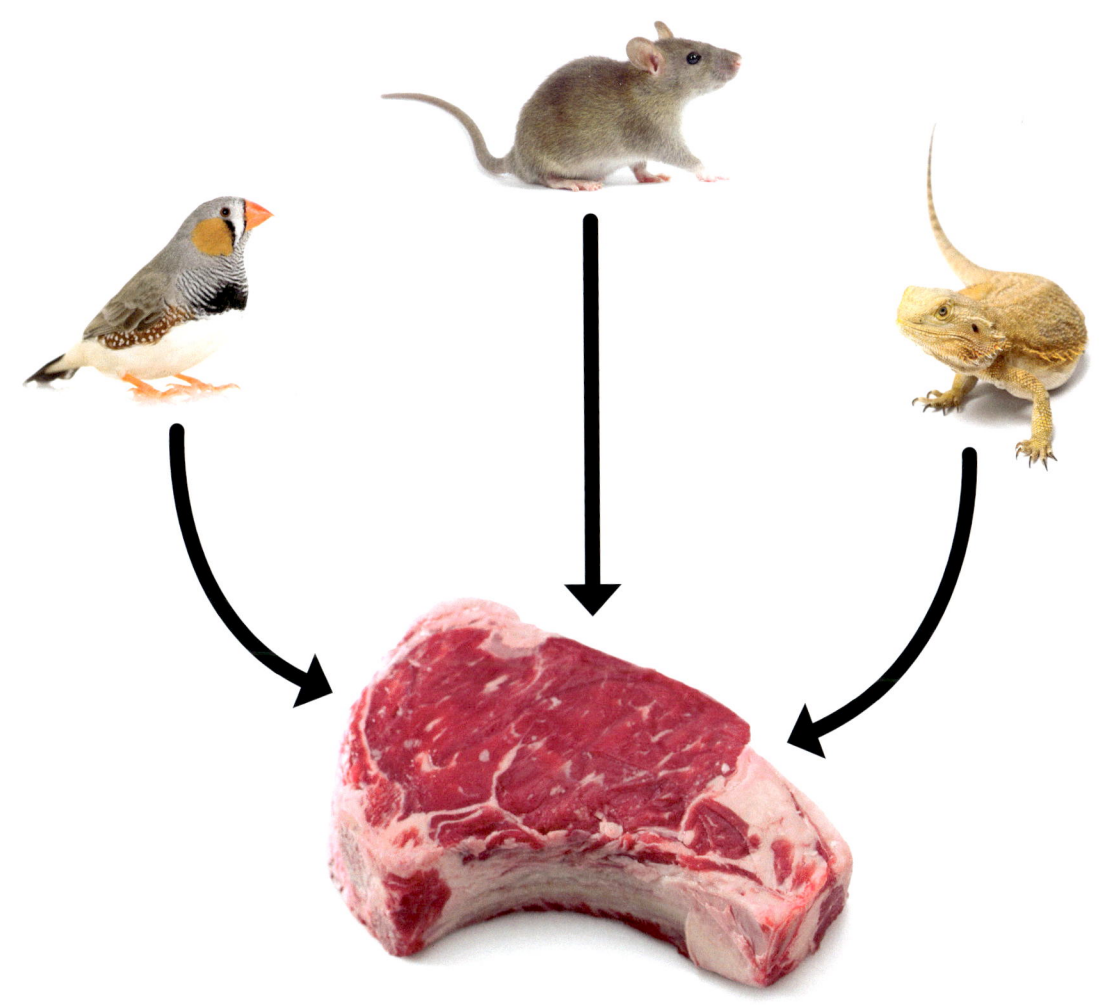

All snakes eat meat.

Lots of snakes get food like this.

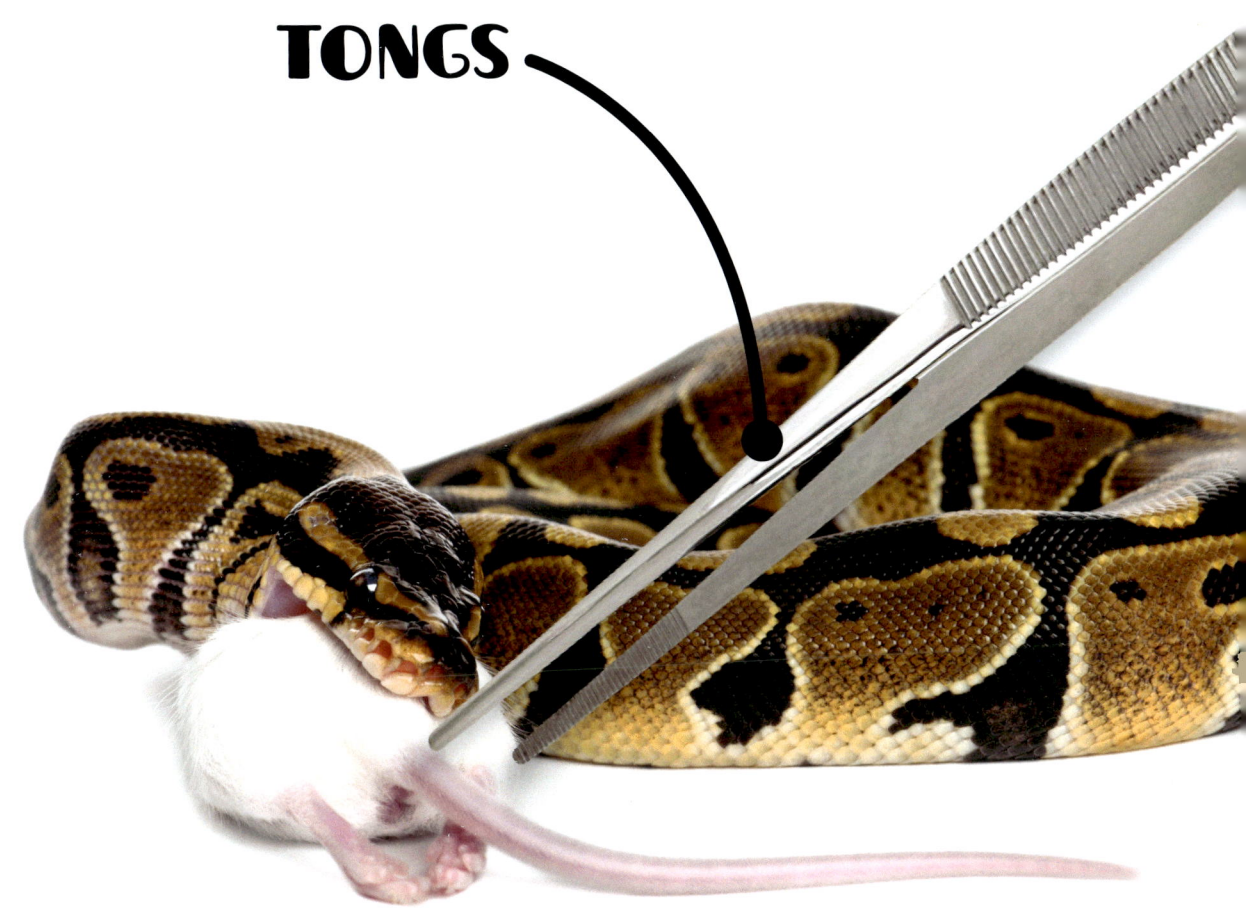

TONGS

My snake can't do that.
He gets food like this.

This is water.

**All snakes have
to have water.**

Lots of snakes get water like this.

WATER BOWL

My snake can't do that. He gets water like this.

Do you want a snake?

Will you get a snake here?

No. They can't live in a house with you.

Get a snake from here.

TANK

They can live with you.

They can make good pets!

Point to the 4 items you need before you can get a pet snake.

tank

water bowl

cage

toys

coat

heat lamp

ball

food

24